HOLOCAUST
EVA MOZES KOR

Author: Hollie Kruse

Copyright © 2024 Vancour

All rights reserved.

DEDICATION

Dedicated to our readers.

BOOK CONTENTS

THE HOLOCAUST	7
WHAT HAPPENED AT AUSCHWITZ	11
AFTER 1945	21
AFTER THE HOLOCAUST	33
EVA MOZES KOR	37
JOSEF MENGELE -THE ANGEL OF DEATH	45
AFTER THE WAR	53

THE HOLOCAUST

Romania and Holocaust

Romania was not occupied but allied with Nazi Germany from 1940 onwards, collaborating with them in policy and in the war. Romania had a long history of anti-Semitism, particularly in the east of the country. Instead of being engaged, Romania teamed up with Nazi Germany and cooperated with them in both politics and the battles. King Carol II stepped down from his role and General Ion Antonescu assumed control of Romania. His Government was called the National Legionary State. Their foundations were built on a basis that was predominately fascist. Other than that, in order to usher their politics, the Iron Guard was also welcomed by them. Like the roots traced, it was fiercely anti-Semitic in nature. The country later joined World War II after merging with the Axis Alliance. Romania was growing with anti-Semitism and that was evident through their support towards the Nazis for capturing the Soviet Union. The authorities of Romania collaborated with the Nazis to organise atrocities against the Jews. They did not step back to execute massively. In addition to that, they even undertook many operations of their own in remote areas or Jews densely populated areas. In this venture, the locals of the country also joined the authorities as they were also anti-Semitic. They brutally killed the Jews of their country. However, this did not proceed long. The party was overthrown by the National Democratic Bloc. The new administration easily parted their ways with Germany by joining with the Soviet Union's settlements.

Torture and Killing

Jews were tortured under the regime of Antonescu. With the actively orchestrated assaults led by The Iron Guard, a vast majority of Jews were killed and attacked. Not only the physical brutalities, they had no rights as a social citizen. Additionally, to further constrain each aspect of Jewish people's needs, the fascist Antonescu government strengthened preceding Nazi ideology laws. They were not permitted to own any kind of property and their businesses were taken over by the government. Also, they were barred from almost all fields of employment and educational institutions as well. The worst part was they were even prohibited from travelling.

Established from Chisinau, the camps flourished more in Romania. Bogdanovka had the camp later. The Holocaust claimed the lives of about 420,000 Jews resided in Romania.

WHAT HAPPENED AT AUSCHWITZ

Auschwitz started off as a facility for holding political criminals and suspects. But it eventually turned into a system of concentration camps where Jews and other individuals who were seen as adversaries of Nazi were murdered, frequently in a chamber filled with poisonous gasses or forced to work as slaves. Auschwitz-Birkenau was a site for convicts; additionally a place targeted in many horrific medical trials carried out by Josef Mengele opened in 1940 and was the largest of the Nazi concentration and death camps. Located in southern Poland, It is estimated that Auschwitz witnessed the death of over one million people. It was around the time of the Second World War. The cruelties halted when Soviet troops showed up there. By the time, Nazi left the camp along with around sixty thousand captives. They were shifted to new sites. In World War II (1939-45), the scenes of Auschwitz shocked the Soviet army when they arrived at the spot. Vast numbers of malnourished prisoners and mountains of bodies were placed there.

The Implementation of Death Camps

Hitler instituted a strategy called the Final Solution right after the Second World War. He was not satisfied with acts against the Jews. He tried to alienate them both in Germany and the nations under their control, imposed upon cruel laws, and brutality against them. He eventually arrived at a conclusion that the best way to deal with them is to exterminate all the Jews from all the firms, like teaching, art, politics and so on, which seemed unsuitable for sustaining in the country. After the start of World War II, Adolf Hitler (1889-1945), the chancellor of Germany from 1933 to 1945", Adolf Hitler commanded the establishment of death camps to carry out this goal. In contrast to detention centres or other camps, these were made for the primary intention of murdering Jews as well as the rest of the convicts during the Holocaust. The ordinary concentration camps, but at the other hand, had prevailed in Germany and served as prison camps for Jews, opposition figures, and certain other individuals regarded as adversaries of the Nazi regime.

The Jewish men under the charge of expelling dead bodies from the chambers and crematoriums even organised a revolt. They destroyed funeral stations and attacked the securities with the weapons. But, the rebels were captured and assassinated in Auschwitz.

The biggest and possibly greatest renowned among all the Nazi concentration camps, Auschwitz, began its operations in the early 1940s. Rudolf Höss, who had formerly assisted in managing the Sachsenhausen concentration camp in Oranienburg, served as its first commander. Auschwitz was built on an ex-army camp outside of Oswiecim, a town in southern Poland close to one of the biggest towns in the nation. Surrounding industries were taken over by the Nazis as the camp was being built, and everyone who lived in the neighbourhood was dragged away from their houses before they were destroyed. When Germany conquered Poland, Auschwitz was initially intended as an ordinary concentration camp to house all of the civilians detained at the time. Activists who were against Nazi, political leaders, fighters, and notable figures from the arts and sciences were among those imprisoned. But as Adolf Hitler's Final Solution became accepted as Nazi doctrine, Auschwitz came to be seen as the prime destination for a killing camp. For starters, it was located close to the geographic centre of all the nations of Europe that were under the German occupation. Another reason was that it was adjacent to the system of railway networks that were used to transfer prisoners to the Nazi camps. Not everyone who reached Auschwitz was executed right away, though. The manufacturing of weapons, vulcanized rubber, and other items regarded as fundamental to Germany's operations in the Second World War. So, they employed slave labour from those judged appropriate for the job.

Auschwitz and Its Subdivisions

Auschwitz had a number of units at its time of function. About twenty thousand political convicts were imprisoned in the first camp, often referred to as Auschwitz I. Its renowned and humorous motto was, "Arbeit Macht Frei,". It means "Work Makes You Free," which welcomes visitors at the main doorway.

Heinrich Himmler was the head of the "Schutzstaffel". Schutzstaffel, known as Select Guard or Protection Squad, is more popularly known as the SS. Heinrich was the head who managed the concentration camps and death camps under Nazi, gave the order to build Auschwitz II near the settlement of Birkenau. In 1941, the largest Auschwitz facility of Birkenau had a capacity of about ninety thousand inmates.

There were also a number of baths where numerous individuals were murdered by poisonous gas and cremated, as well as furnaces for burning the dead. At Auschwitz II, the bulk of Auschwitz inmates perished. The area was littered with far more than forty limited facilities, known as sub camps that acted as slave labour camps. Around ten thousand inmates were kept in Monowitz, which is the biggest of these sub camps and also referred to as Auschwitz III, which began operation in 1942.

The Treatment in Auschwitz

Jews were accounted for the largest proportion of those deported to Auschwitz camps. The Nazi physicians inspected prisoners after they arrived at the camp. The sick, kids, pregnant ladies among the inmates deemed unworthy for employment, and they were all given the go-ahead to take showers. As it is said the bathrooms they made, however, were actually secret gas chambers. The inmates were administered Zyklon-B which is a toxic and dangerous gas when they got in. Unsuited for labour individuals have never been formally recognised as Auschwitz prisoners. The amount of people perished in the camp cannot be determined for this reason.

Large numbers of the inmates who originally avoided the torture of chambers passed perished as a result of exhaustion, illness, inadequate nourishment, or the constant fight to survive under appalling circumstances. Regular punishment, abuse, and cruel killings took place in the presence of the rest of the captives.

Certain of the captives at Birkenau were the subjects of cruel clinical research. German physician Josef Mengele, who started working at Auschwitz in 1943, was the main instigator of this heinous study. Mengele conducted several tests on prisoners. For instance, he painfully shot serum into the eyes of several youngsters in order to examine eye colour. Additionally, he gave twins chloroform injections into their hearts to see if their deaths would occur simultaneously and in a similar way.

Holocaust Tale of Eva Mozes Kor

AFTER 1945

The Auschwitz camp commanding officers started erasing records of the atrocities that had occurred there as 1944 was coming to an end and it appeared that the Allies would beat Nazi. Documents were rubbed out; constructions were burned down, blasted up, or blazed to the ground.

It was in 1945 January, the Nazis decided to vacate the camp from Auschwitz as they knew of the arrival of the Soviet team. About sixty thousand prisoners were ordered to leave the camp and made to travel thirty kilometres from there. It was later referred to as the Auschwitz death marches. Many inmates perished in the act, and those who survived were transported by rail to prison camps in Germany. Finally, in January, the Soviet troops invaded Auschwitz camp and discovered over seven thousand six hundred ill or malnourished prisoners who had been abandoned there. Furthermore, the army found heaps of dead bodies, pairs of footwear and garments, as well as seven tonnes of hair which had been removed from prisoners prior to their execution. Approximately one and a half million individuals, the large numbers of whom were Jews, perished at Auschwitz throughout its duration of existence, as per different reports.

On January 27, 1945, the allied forces invaded the Auschwitz concentration camps and saw a horrific scene of mass murder. Never before had our planet seen anything like it. After Germany invaded Poland and started World War II, the SS, also known as the shot stuffle, turned Auschwitz I into a prisoner of war camp. Later, the building of Auschwitz II Birkenau, the scene of untold crimes, began. 1.1 million Of the 1.3 million individuals sent to Auschwitz died there and had their bodies desecrated. That number is startling all by itself. But when survivors revealed the horrifying reality of what had actually transpired, the public would soon be stunned even more. Hitler would pursue a campaign of mass annihilation that had been advocated by several right-wing radicals before him when he became the Chancellor of Germany from 1933 to 1945. And this Nazi ideology's approach to policy became recognised as the definitive answer to the Jewish problem. Germany already possessed a number of concentration camps that served as incarceration facilities for Jews, political prisoners, and other adversaries of the Nazi regime before World War II began. But these were only hints at what was to follow, not the whole story. In Polish army barracks, the Nazis established detention camps as they conquered Poland. The construction of this first camp was overseen by the renowned Rudolf Hoss, who also served as the camp's inaugural commander. Auschwitz was apparently picked because it was at the intersection of forty four parallel tracks or railway lines, which could be utilised to conveniently transport war captives.

Rudolf Hoss would also direct the building of a crematorium that was initially planned to be used to burn the remains of condemned inmates or other deceased people. However, by May 1942, three furnaces that could burn 340 people in twenty four hours had been erected, and they were being used to murder even the captives who were still alive. In this sense, the crematoriums would represent the Nazi regime's cruelty and contempt for human life. These chambers would be followed by four more, for a total of five, when the Nazis continued construction. Hitler visited the camp in March 1941 and gave the order to enlarge it so that even more prisoners could be sent to Auschwitz. Due to this, a new camp, known as Auschwitz II Birkenau was built near to the first camp and was finished in October 1941. About fifteen thousand prisoners of war might have been housed in the original camp. While Birkenau could house over ninety thousand, this startling figure demonstrated how the Nazi tyranny was only just beginning and ensured that Birkenau would become the scene of numerous horrors against the human race. Nearly 1.1 million of the 1.3 million overall prisoners of war were Jews, making the largest proportion of the detainees. The two lakh additional inmates were mostly non-Jewish Poles, Roma, Gypsies, homosexuals, Soviet POWs, and those who were psychologically unfit to be utilised in Hitler's master plan for Europe. The extent of the horrible death and torture perpetrated on the prisoners of war is difficult to conceive and much harder to comprehend, making it one of the worst disasters in global history. When the Soviet Red Army arrived at Auschwitz, they discovered a huge collection of shoes that the victims of this cruel catastrophe had left behind.

At Auschwitz, prisoners would arrive crammed into cattle wagons in the worst conditions imaginable. But, what waited for them was even worse. On their arrival, they would be given triangular pieces of clothes which were sewn into their jackets above their prisoner number. By July 1942, a large portion of those sent to the camps at Auschwitz were Jewish descent. These victims would be examined by Nazi doctors and those who they considered unfit for work or duty were immediately sent to take a shower in bathrooms. But, these showers would be of a lethal kind and these bathrooms were actually disguised gas chambers. As this was just a method to whittle down the number of unfit prisoners. These would include young children, elderly couples, pregnant women, and the mentally or physically infirm. Once the unfit prisoners would be inside the gas chambers, they would be exposed to a lethal poison gas called Cyclone b.

The biggest tragedy surrounding this entire episode was that these prisoners were never registered in the Nazi database and therefore, it is impossible to find out the true extent of horrible atrocities committed against the weak and the old. Political prisoners would wear a red triangle sewn into their shirts, while German criminals would have a green piece, Prostitutes, gypsies and the Roma would wear black and homosexual would wear pink. Jews would be forced to wear a yellow badge in the design of the Star of David and in this way prisoners would be differentiated into various factions. Furthermore, the nationality of a particular inmate was indicated by a letter stitched into their clothing. Because of this differentiation, a racial hierarchy began to be formed with German prisoners at the top, followed by non-Jewish prisoners from various countries, while the Jewish prisoners would be at the bottom. Those who survived the initial gas chambers would be forced into a life of slavery where many would die from over exhaustion, lack of nutrition and many more would succumb to the daily struggle. That was life in Auschwitz.

For the men, the day would begin at 4.30 a.m., with the women rising up even earlier when the block supervisor would ring a gong signalling the start of daily labour and slavery. The block supervisor would go around beating the inmates with a stick in order to make them use the latrine quickly. The sanitary arrangements were of course absolutely horrible and led to many infections and diseases. For their breakfast prisoners would only receive five hundred milligrams of coffee substitute in order to keep them working.

After this, a second gong would be wrung in order to call all of the inmates outside and make them stand in neat rows of Tens. So, they could be counted. These inmates would be forced to stand outside for hours on end until the SS officers came for the count. After recounting and making sure every prisoner was present, work would commence. No rest periods were allowed and even the latrine breaks would be recorded so that the officers could completely control every free second of the inmates' lives. Lunch would be served at midday and consisted of a watery soup that was reported to be disgausting and unhygienic. The evening meal would be a measly three hundred grams of bread which was mostly mouldy and unfit for eating. After the day's work would end a second roll call would take place where floggings and hangings were common. Many would be punished for any infractions that they might have caused. If any prisoner was missing, the rest would be forced to stand in roll call until and unless the missing prisoner in question was found. At night time, the prisoners exhausted from the hellish labour and the ruthlessness of their Nazi officers would go to rest and receive their mail. Jewish prisoners would not be allowed any mail and thus were even kept deprived of any family news on the outside. For sleep, thousands of prisoners would be forced into a single wooden or brick barrack and as soon as the night-time curfew gong was sounded, Auschwitz would go completely silent. In the darkness of night, only one madman will continue his experiments. That mad man Joseph Mengele, who known as Angel of Death, for his cruel and inhumane experiments on Jewish prisoners. He would do experiments on babies, no older than a few months old and it was his genocide nature that prolonged the suffering of hundreds of thousands of victims. The right of terror is long and frightening but it too must come to a close and give way to the light of the morning sun.

In 1945, the Soviet army entered Auschwitz finding approximately 7800 sick detainees. While an estimated sixty thousand had been sent on the gruelling death march where many would lose their lives. More than a million would lose their lives in this horrific tragedy. The pain and sacrifices of those people should never be forgotten.

AFTER THE HOLOCAUST

Germany was in upheaval upon losing the First World War. They felt disgraced in the eyes of the global community, their administration was useless, and they were going through a severe economic downturn. People of the country were jobless, in need of, and starved. The Organizations that were formed made a lot of claims about having the solution to the national issues. The majority of those were fiercely against democracy, the haters of Jews and intensely nationalistic. Adolf enrolled in the National Socialist German Worker's Party, among several other organisations that later gained notoriety. His charismatic nature and skill as a great orator contributed to the group's expansion. They even attempted to overthrow the administration in the middle of the 1920s, but they were unsuccessful. It was during his stay in the prison, Hitler composed Mein Kampf. It means My Struggle. Even though he received a five jail term, he only spent nine months inside the prison. Hitler's book became the holy book of the Nazis. It explains the beliefs and development prospects that the party should implement when they came into force, however it is incredibly tedious and hard to comprehend. Adolf Hitler had a preoccupation with ethnicity and racial integrity. He believed that the Jewish community was the most subpar and that the Aryans were greater to all others. He used derogatory terms for describing Jews including "worm," "maggot," "vermin," and "snake". He believed that he could have won the battle if some dishonest Hebrew were killed. And the Tragedy is proof that he truly meant everything he stated. But it's crucial to keep in mind that he wasn't the only one who might have killed numerous Jews. He must have had a lot of helpers and spectators who shared his Jew hating views.

Holocaust Tale of Eva Mozes Kor

EVA MOZES KOR

The Voice of the Survivor

The survivors and witnesses of the holocaust are life-long traumatised. Eva Kor is not simply a historical footnote. She is a survivor of the Auschwitz atrocities and pseudoscientific experiments. Among the abuses given by Nazis, Eva Kor and her sister Miriam were supposed to have undergone cruel experiments under Doctor Josef Menegele. They were one of the twins who Josef Mengele employed in trials to create the ideal Aryan gen. The Romanian born veteran fighted her fate in turn forgiving her cruel abusers. She later evolved into a Sentinel on guard of the past. She spoke for forgiveness a lot. According to her, it is only for healing and empowerment. She referred to it as a magical drug, which heals a man and will not give any negative impacts and it is effective as well. Kor overcame a difficult time in the past and is working to leave a legacy that is forgiving. After she had recovered, she recalled the episode and claimed that it all made to her would have killed her. Forgiveness and redemption are considered with high esteem in the aspect of the repercussions resulting from the Holocaust. Even so, the literature dealing with psychology rarely occupies the fact of its therapeutic benefits. It is indeed found that forgiveness is what helps in fostering a general idea of wellness after human induced traumas. It in turn resulted in resolving the stress and depression. The life of Kor can be studied as a subject that instructs many lessons to be applied in practical life situations, particularly in the current social contexts of people dealing with severe psychological illness and struggles. The Menegele twin's trauma was not simple, but complex. After being freed from the camp, the survivor decided to forgive her abusers. In that context, the case of Kor becomes relevant. She used to dream of horrific experiences. The dead bodies, the dirty condition, unhygienic and terrible food of the camp haunted her for long. Her scenario was exceptional in terms of the innovation. It induces the alteration or transformation with significant degrees of personal and spiritual assimilation. After being lived as a victim and later as a survivor and finally forgiving the abusers, Eva discovered the way to a peaceful life.

Who Was Eva?

Eva was born on January 31, 1934 as the daughter of Alexander Mozes and Jaffia Mozes; she grew up in Portz, Kingdom of Romania. She, her twin Miriam and two siblings, Edit and Aliz along with their parents left for Auschwitz in 1944. Eva was only ten at that time. Eva and Miriam were taken to many experiments since they were twins. Unfortunately, the rest of their family died in the concentration camp. Kor recounted her experiences in the camp. They were kept without clothes for many hours for assessing and measuring. It was incredibly humiliating. She even experienced a severe infection following one of the test injections. After examining her on the following day, they finalised that Kor will survive only a few weeks. But, fate was otherwise. She was on the verge of death, but however, resisted passing away. It would have been pathetic that if Kor died, then Miriam would be murdered so that they could perform a post mortem to analyse their bodily changes.

From What She Said?

From a very young age, she had the potential and courage to resist and overcome. To her family where her father was expecting a boy child since the boy of the family only had the right to perform the religious rituals and she was born. She was really smart and always had arguments with her father unlike her siblings. It was like training for her in the future, to survive and resist. Theirs was a happy family in Romania; her educated mother was really a lovable person who always helped her neighbours. She often described the beautiful small house and their farming they had there. The people of their country were mostly anti-Semitic. When their life became miserable there, her father insisted to leave and migrate to Palestine. As her mother was not willing, they chose to stay there. It was the time when Adolf Hitler became the ruler of Germany and his implementations against the Jews spread towards the rest of Europe as well. When Kor was about six years old, the north of Transylvania was given to Hungary and the people were in danger.

Kor and her sister were even bullied for being Jews. They were kids and in their school, their friends accused them of faults and the teacher punished them. When she explained her situation, her helpless mother advised them to just suffer since they are Jews. This made lil Kor angry. But, her mother's words proved to be true later. The Hungarian Nazi party along with the villagers threw tomatoes and rocks at their house and even called them curse words. The party and army were there to stalk and attack them. One fine night, Kor's father prepared with his family to escape from there. But, they were caught. Thus, they lose all their hopes. Later, they were taken from the village and no one in their village reacted. In Simleul Silvaniei, they were forced to stay in a ghetto. Ghettos were specially made for Jews. They were kept in the fenced areas to torture. Thereafter, the guards transported them from there. The new stay was much more horrific. She witnessed children and people crying, pleading and suffering a lot. Kor, Miriam and their mother were dropped at a concentration camp in Auschwitz, near the town of Oswiecim. Soon after reaching the spot, the SS guards spotted them as twins and they were forcefully taken from their mother. Their dress was taken off, cut their hair and made them take showers. On their dresses red crosses were imprinted. The kids were tattooed then. Kor was tattooed as A-7063 and Miriam was numbered as A-7064.

The twins stayed at Camp II B in Birkenau. It is also known as Auschwitz II. It was actually Joseph Menegele's lab.

JOSEF MENGELE -THE ANGEL OF DEATH

Josef Mengele was brought up in the Bavarian village. It was while working with Professor Otmar Freiherr von Verschuer; he expanded his idea regarding genes and researched more about it. The Gunzburg born positioned as the genetic scientist in the Nazi camp of Auschwitz. Even though he originally intended to utilise his educational qualifications to improve the society and people, the authorities instead exploited it to implement their perspectives.

The concerned team were instructed to get twins for the research conducted by Mengele. They helped him in the venture and subjected about nine hundred such children to carry out his studies. The children were given special treatment like supplying excess meals, keeping naked and all. When the rest of them were killed, these kids were not but, received a much harsher destiny. Exempt from being beaten, children kept for Menegele's experiment were made to do labours, and randomly chosen to take part in risky and frequently lethal treatments in their labs.

Upon reaching the spot of Menegele's experiment site, the children will be made to explain their history and their assessments including the weight and measurements will be taken. Their blood was collected each day in order to hand it over to Professor von Verschuer. They were tested on many medicines and chemicals to know whether they cure the diseases. For that, initially they will be injected with potentially fatal diseases like Scarlet fever. Later, they will be administered with dosages of different substances to check whether it healed their illness. The cruellest part was his way of doing surgeries. Operations were carried and cuts and wounds were made out by keeping them conscious. Deaths of children frequently occurred as a result of these kinds of trials and experiments. Once one of the twins gets killed, then the other will be murdered in order to evaluate the differences in their body and organs by taking post mortems.

The Menegele's lab treated the kids as human guinea pigs. Menegel's aim or purpose was to know how to make blue eyed and blond haired children. The so-called Aryan race was the Master Race for Hilter and he wanted to enhance their numbers. Other than this, they also needed to know the reasons behind abnormalities. They selected those who are handicapped and suffer other issues. Menegele wanted to test some gender exchange as well. The experiments he made for that had killed many children. He exchanged the blood between boys and girls, he even cut the genitals to make them transform. The sole source of relaxation or entertainment for the kids was knitting. Eva also learned it from the other inmates. The continuous exposure to the bromide and other chemicals reduced their ability to memorise and recollect.

The Twin Hunt

The story told by the inmates shocked the kids. The odoured and stinky place had a crematorium and a gas chamber. People were killed and burned there. When Kor was supposed to use the latrine, she was exhausted. The smell of vomiting and feces, along with dead bodies were placed there. Making them seated without clothes among everybody was the worst thing to do. The kids' hair got removed and they suffered because of lices. The authorities placed the kids in a white liquid which used to give them a burning sensation. Even the chemicals fell into their eyes which harmed them. The treatments made them weak and skinny. Menegele used to refer to the kids as his children. Kor never expressed her pain, she never wanted to make the authorities or the enemies realise that their treatments made her weak. She was such a determinant kid. She saw the sacrifice and abuse as the payment for one more day to survive in the world.

When Kor was deeply ill after multiple injections, she had only one thing in her mind. She might not be the reason for her sister's death. They knew that the sick children who were transported from there would not come back. However, Eva survived all those. The authorities almost predicted and confirmed her death. After years, Eva recollected what Menegele said as the young girl had two weeks left. It's not known whether the undefeatable spirit and mental strength of the ten years old child made her survive. Anyways, her comeback made Menegele cancel the plan to inject chloroform to Miriam's heart. Then, she would have gone through the post mortem procedures to compare the bodily changes with Eva Mozes. Theft and attempts to escape were the crimes and those who tried it would be perished. In January 1945, they were forced to leave there. Eva, her sister and some of the twins chose to stay there. The Nazis hurriedly left from there. They managed to survive there with some clothes and food. The SS guards attacked them again, but the people hid and stayed there in the camp. After days of attack, the Nazi quit. The Soviet soldiers came there to rescue them and served them chocolates. She came to be called the woman in blue.

She shared the word about the Holocaust and that would never forget it across Indiana and the rest of the world. But also discover how to forgive. Kor subsequently made Terre Haute her home. She was visiting the detention camp where she was kept as a kid. She visited Auschwitz, the Nazi concentration camp, multiple times throughout the years. She and her twin sister Miriam were there when Nazi Dr. Joseph Menegele, the so-called angel of death, put them to the horrifying and barbaric ordeal. They both did, however, live. When the camp was freed, they were ten years old. The only survivors in her immediate family were Eva and Miriam. She subsequently relocated to Israel, where she married another survivor, and the couple then came to Terre Haute. She inaugurated the CANDLES museum there in 1995. Children of Auschwitz Nazi Deadly love experiments survivors are shortly known as CANDLE. In Terre Haute, Eva ran the holocaust museum.

Holocaust Tale of Eva Mozes Kor

AFTER THE WAR

When the war was over, Eva and Miriam lived in Romania and did their schooling. At the age of eighteen, both got the opportunity to leave the country and they migrated to Israel, like their parents told them earlier. Upon reaching there, Kor and Miriam served in the army. Kor spent eight years in the army and she was promoted to the role of Sergeant Major in the Israeli Army Engineering Corps. Later, she got married to Michael Kor. Michael was also a survivor like Eva and the couple lived in the United States after that. She found some sort of relief after getting such a partner as he had similar experiences of a twin and a survivor of the holocaust. They resided in Terre Haute. There she became subjected to bullying as her behaviour irritated the neighbours. Her childhood trauma affected her physical health much later. She even donated her kidney to her sister, but she unfortunately died of kidney cancer.

Eva started getting appreciation and admiration from all over the world after interviews and the series Holocaust casting Meryl Streep and James Woods came out. The twin sisters then started looking for the experimentation victims in 1978. In 1984, Eva established her foundation CANDLES which expanded as "Children of Auschwitz Nazi Deadly Lab Experiments Survivors" in 1984. Eva became the head of the foundation and was involved in the group till her death. She founded the foundation by herself when the rest of the survivors did not respond.

Ten years later, she assisted in the opening of the Terre Haute CANDLES Holocaust Museum and Education Centre, which was later ruined in 2003. In 2005, a brand-new facility debuted. She was an exceptionally sharp speaker who was straightforward and persuasive. Heberer Rice remarked that Eva had a gift for expressing whatever she experienced at the moment in a highly subtle and sensitive manner.

Holocaust Tale of Eva Mozes Kor

She was not widely praised for her act to forgive Mengele and other abusers. However, the decision of Eva and her remark persisted. Although, that this was a method for her to deal with her misfortune and carry on with her future.

Robert Enright, Eva's one of the acquaintances, commented that by forgiving, no one is compromising or undermining justice. It does not imply endorsing or even making amends. He explained it with the analogy that a thief can be given some money and can be forgiven. Not repeating the act is wise. Kor won several honours for her support of mercy, beginning in 1985 when she was named News Woman of the Year by the Israeli Press.

'Surviving the Angel of Death: The True Story of a Mengele Twin in Auschwitz' is a work that Kor authored for children to share about her encounters there. The people demand vengeance and there is a significant hurdle to forgiveness for most individuals. She says, It appears that we must pay tribute to our martyrs, but she frequently questions if her deceased family and loved ones would have wanted her to endure agony and resentment till her death.

She bore the burden of Auschwitz. She had the trauma of losing her family at the age of ten. Later, the twin sisters suffered a lot and survived. However, she chose what really meant for her and passed on her strength acquired from history and experiences.

Eva made her trip back to Auschwitz in 1984. There she vowed to share the history of Eva's family. The potential of Eva and the determination she showed up was astonishing when she yelled 'bloody murder' about her abuser, Mengele. She became irritated once his remnants were not fully discovered. She had the courage to protest against this at the meeting attended by the American authorities. It was in 1990; Eva officially pardoned every Nazis, even the fellow abuser Joseph Mengele and the ruler Hitler. It sparked so much more criticism. Although Eva made it clear that she was just advocating for herself, her organisation and attempts for pardoning others ended up being the centrepiece of her heritage. Up until the moment of her passing, Kor was quite busy giving visits to Auschwitz and teaching and exhibiting all over the world. She frequently brought colleagues and the representatives of the organization with her when she visited Auschwitz. Eva sued Bayer for the involvement in the cruel human testing experimentation that took place at the concentration camps. The parties deal reached after receiving $5 billion for Memory, Commitment, and Future.

She collaborated with the state representatives Tim Skinner and Clyde Kersey to enact a bill mandating Holocaust education in secondary schools. Kor was also included in the CNN documentaries "Voices of Auschwitz" and "Incredible survivors". She went to Germany to give a witness statement in the case of former Nazi member Oskar Gröning, the bookkeeper. Both of them hugged and kissed all across the hearing, with Kor expressing thanks to Gröning for his readiness to testify at the age of ninety three about what took place more than a decade back. In 2016, The Girl Who Forgave the Nazis, a British documentary by Channel 4, came out which featured Eva. It covers Eva and Groening's encounter. Being one of Thirteen Victims of the holocaust who participated in the USC Shoah Foundation's New Dimension in Testimony technology project which as in 2016, Eva was able to respond to all the queries as if she or he were physically present. After she passed away, Lesley Stahl spoke with her avatar on the TV news show for an hour. At Butler University situated in Indianapolis, Eva: A-7063, in the form of a documentary, had its grand opening in 2018. Ed Asner performed as the narrator, and it includes conversations with Elliott Gould, a number of historians, and individuals from Eva's life. The PBS network has aired it. As a grownup, Eva Mozes came to the realization that she needed to forgive those who had mistreated her in the encampments in order for the reason that she could recover. She wrote letters to the people who had harmed her for months. Even Menegele received a letter from her. Although she found it extremely difficult to compose them, she thought that doing so made her a better and more productive individual. She thought that forgiving was beneficial for her and the proper act to do, even though not all pleased with her plans and deeds.

Both of the twins were made to endure abuse and laboratory experimentation by Dr. Joseph Mengele, the so-called "angel of death". Mirriam died in 1993. They were given shots of mysterious substances, which for Miriam, Kor's twin, would never be known, and would cause her death long after the liberation of Auschwitz.

Kor passed away on July 4, 2019, while travelling to Auschwitz with the CANDLES group members from Poland. At that time, she was eighty five. She travelled there every year to talk about her early life and lead trips from the viewpoint of a survivor. On 12 July, Kor was featured in the BBC Radio 4 obituary programme Last Word. Four governors of Indiana honoured Eva Mozes Kor. She received the Sagamore of the Wabash Award, with the Distinguished Hoosier Award from Indiana. Also, in 2017 she received the same award with the Sachem Award, which is the state's highest award. Additionally she was chosen for Grand Marshal of the Indianapolis five hundred Festival Parade in April 2017. She was awarded the Doctor of Humane Letters by Butler University in 2015. Furthermore, during the same year, she was given the 2015 Mike Vogel Humanitarian Award, the Anne Frank Change the World Award, and the Wabash Valley Women of Influence Award. Kor was recognised for her perseverance, empathy, and kindness in the light of bigotry and violence at the 24th Annual ADL in Concert against Hate in 2018. The Indiana State Teachers Association presented her with the "Friend of Education" award posthumously in 2020. She has won more than thirty honours from colleges, governments, and non-profits in total, plus three doctorates. After Kor passed away in 2019, an art with her distinctive peace symbol was made. Kor's fifty three foot-tall image is meant to contrast with her little height. She was supposed to appear bigger than real, according to the individuals who ordered the artwork. Her portrait stands beside those of other significant Indiana personalities including Mari Evans and Kurt Vonnegut. In November of 2020, the work was finished.

She made it her goal to disseminate the idea that adversity and sorrow can be overcome and that forgiving others may aid in our recovery. The difficulties Eva Kor surmounted and the teachings she imparted to people everywhere. Holocaust made death seem so simple. According to Eva Mozes Kor in her book, 'Surviving the Angel of Death: The True Story of a Mengele Twin in Auschwitz', survival was a comprehensive task. Everyone has obstacles, she notes, but everyone should concentrate on the prospect of long-term success. Together with Miriam, she overcame Nazi repression. She stated, describing her life, that she didn't want people prying into her soul further. For her, it was a lot of effort, and they probe into her core. She wasn't quite prepared for sharing her experiences anymore. She nonetheless made the trip in an effort to educate others regarding the Holocaust. She has made it her life's work to forgive her tormentors all across the world.

She relocated to Terre Haute, with her husband despite the fact that she does not speak English. People mocked her since the people of Terre Haute were not familiar with her tale. She also struggled with how to effectively describe whatever has occurred to her. As a result, she experienced anti-Semitic jokes while living there and was the victim of a racist attack. After some time, she managed to find her words. Much more controversially, she eventually decided to publicly forgive the Nazi abusers.

In order to find and encourage twin victims who had also been tortured under Mengele, Kor founded CANDLES in 1984. CANDLES transformed into a museum with a goal of educating people about the Holocaust in 1995. She discovered one hundred and twenty two other twin victims throughout her quest. She soon started covering the costs of the instructors who joined her on the future journeys. She has occasionally conducted trips to her mother country Romania and has also conducted visits to Auschwitz as well.

Mengele was able to avoid jail time for the following thirty years after the war, but then officials received information that brought them to his tomb which was in Brazil, where he had drowned accidently died years previously. He tried to escape to South America and died in 1979. In terms of modern bioethical concern, Mengele's history eventually pointed them in the direction of the maxim that all doctors adhere not to do any damage or evil.

From her experiences, she says to hold on to your dreams and life will serve the best things. And treat people depending on their behaviours and actions.

According to Eva, being distinctive is not a result of what individuals can do to oneself on the outside or other factors, such as what they put on. One's strongest internal capabilities and how he or she interacts with the outside realm determine how distinctive he or she is. It will not originate from a tattoo or a high-end garment. Eva had left a large number of messengers. According to Alex Kor, her son, many of them will travel and give speeches about his mum. He believes that as the manner or method to persist the messages she had given.

The survivors, who lived after being freed, continue to share their tale in the faith that their misfortune would never be reproduced. Kor inaugurated the CANDLES Holocaust Museum and Education Centre in 1995. In addition to contributing to publications, she has delivered more than three thousand talks throughout the globe. By sharing the life experiences she has discovered through her suffering, she aimed to inspire others to forgive the harshest adversary and forgive anyone who has been wounded. Then that will cure the spirit and bring peace.

Printed in Great Britain
by Amazon